HOW TO RUN YOUR OWN

SEO

COMPANY

Amateurs to Professionals

Paden Clayton

ISBN-13: 978-1532762529

ISBN-10: 1532762526

This book is dedicated to my wife who has been there through all the long work hours, the meetings during dinner, and all the work that has gone into this book. This is also dedicated to my daughter Sam who worked with me on fixing the countless issues from bad transcriptioning services.

Thank you for your support and love over the years.

Contents

How to Run a SEO Business...1

What This Book Is...3

Methodology...5

SEO Color Chart...7

Business Advice..11

    Banking... 12

    Payments.. 13

    Contracts.. 16

    Website... 17

What is SEO?...19

Types of SEO...21

Training...23

Before Starting SEO..25

    Gather Information from your Client............................25

    Paperwork and Payments..30

Performing SEO...33

    The Research Stage...33

    The Manual Method..33

    Using Paid Tools 35

    Baseline Analysis..36

    Notes on making changes...41

    Beginning the Changes...42

    Working with Content Management Systems...............42

    HTML Sites...44

Handling Reorganization Properly......................................45

Optimizing the Page Content..46

Conversion Rate Optimization..49

Ads or Pay Per Click Campaigns.......................................49

Keeping Track of Clients and Reporting...........................51

Paid Subscription Tools...52

Backlinks...55

What They Are, and Why We Want Them........................55

How to Get Them..56

Copying Competitor's Backlinks......................................56

Researching Your Own Backlinks.....................................58

What to Watch Out For...59

Wrapping Things Up...61

Resources..63

How to Run a SEO Business

ow to run a Search Engine Optimization (SEO) business seems like it's a common question these days. There are so many companies out there constantly offering services on how to optimize your site, boost your rankings and trying to earn you more money through your website overall.

With all the money that's included in this, you might be asking yourself things like "how do I get into this business?", "How do I perform SEO?", or "How do I offer these same services to other companies?"

I want to start by personally thanking you for purchasing this book, and taking the time to read it. Throughout the course of this book we are actually going to touch base on multiple sections. We're going to go in detail on how to actually perform SEO, what SEO is, items like keyword research, SEO management and how it all ties together to actually form SEO. We are going to talk about good SEO, bad SEO and which route you should actually go for. We are also going to talk about actually educating yourself and your client on SEO.

What This Book Is

This book is designed for people that have a little bit of computer knowledge. People that are not afraid of trying out new applications, learning new information, and for the folks that want to get deep into SEO.

Methodology

The methodology that we're going to recommend during this is has three core points:

Honesty

Knowledge

Follow up

Honesty is definitely the most important factor when it comes to working with your clients. The more honest you are with your clients, the more honest they are going to be with you. This raises the chances that they will trust you with the work, and at the end of the day everything will run smoother because of that.

For knowledge, when people come to you for for SEO, or when you're offering these services you are often viewed as a leader in your market area of SEO and optimization. Keeping this in mind, when a client asks you a question you will need to be able to answer the question or have the resources for the information. Coming back to our first core point, don't try to shrug off a question or make it seem like you know the information if you really don't. Be honest with the client by letting him or her know "Hey, I'm not quite sure about that so let me do some research into it for the proper information". You can then come back to the client and they will definitely appreciate your honestly and the extra steps you took to help them, instead of trying to pull one over on them.

As you are performing SEO and after you have completed SEO you should frequently follow up your clients to ensure they understand the process, to make sure you understand their needs and goals, and to make sure to you are working towards reaching those goals together.

SEO Color Chart

When it comes to SEO, sometimes you'll hear about the different colors of SEO. So when dealing with the colors of SEO it is helpful to relate them to the representative colors of hacking. That connotation is a little rough, but it really is a similar example. There are white hat, black hat, and gray hat hackers. In this situation, the same explanation goes for both SEO and hacking.

"White hat" basically means you are doing everything by the book. You strictly follow all the rules, and refuse to break any of them. You're doing everything exactly the way that it's supposed to be done, and not veering outside of the box.

The "Black hat" description means that you're doing things in a way that kind of walks a fine line. Option A could lead to a lot of client traffic, or option B could lead to being blacklisted from Google, and completely disappearing from search engines. Your services could disappear from Bing or

Yahoo just as easily. When something like that happens, it leads to starting all over again. When dealing with black hats, you're typically going to be looking at links paying for links, using automated software blog commenting, account creations, automatic sharing, and things like that required. That's not to say all software deals with black hat colors, but there is a lot of software out in the world that does.

"Grey hat" means you're typically doing some of each. You do work by the book to see if it makes sense and you feel comfortable doing it, then you can use automated tools. In the grey hat area you typically see people taking a very conservative nature towards their work. Gray hats are extremely careful as they understand the possibility and risks of getting caught and blacklisted. On the contrary, you have an increase in the possibility of getting higher search ranks when working as a grey hat because you're using certain automation and speeding the process up.

Before you dive into SEO, you should really consider which hat you want to wear. This book is geared more towards the white hat area, and it's the area we would recommend. However, if you do decide you are interested in the black hat or grey hat area there is a lot of information out there to help get started on that. This is where you generally see tools like SENuke, or other tools similar to that in which there is a lot of automation. There you'll see things such as spintax, and other information like that.

Once you have figured out which area you want to follow you will have to create your plans for the future, and understand how to work with a client. If you are in the black hat area we recommend letting your client know that there is a possibility of being blacklisted in the future. We understand if you choose not to do that as it could turn clients away, but at the same time you are risking yourself to liability by getting a client's site completely removed from search engines and damaging their reputation and finances.

Business Advice

Similar to any other business, SEO has a business of its own. There are a lot of rules and regulations that you would want to follow to make it easier on yourself. You want to be aware of tax situations and liabilities when setting your business up. Are you going to go with the sole proprietorship, where the taxes come back on yourself? Are you going to set up a corporation, an LLC, or a partnership? In either case all the same business rules still apply. If you are doing this as free-lance work, depending on how you are managing your business, you might have to deal in situations where clients treat you similar to an employee or contractor. It depends on how you choose to set your work up. For ease of use, I'd recommend the sole proprietorship option if you're just starting off by yourself. Once you collect a little more money you can move into the LLC side of things and try to protect yourself a bit better. If you don't mind the extra work and headaches, or if you're functioning a larger business the corporation side of things is always an option.

Banking

After the basic business is set up, you can then move on to how the finances for your business should function. <u>If you've already got a business set up, feel free to skip over this section</u>. You will usually want to keep a separate bank account or multiple bank accounts for your business. A helpful set up we generally recommend is a bank that supports multiple accounts or subaccounts. Now, with typical banks you will have to pay a fee to open multiple accounts. You can however use something like Ally Bank, which is based completely online.

There's no minimum deposit for individual accounts so you can create multiple individual accounts. On the downside, when dealing with something like Ally Bank they don't offer business accounts so these would be personal accounts. There are other bank accounts that you can use the same method with. What it basically consists of is you creating multiple accounts for your money to be organized and deposited into. You might have one bank account in which your money is deposited into, and from there you can determine where it should go. Maybe you decide to have a separate account for paying bills. You will want to have a separate account for recurring costs. Maybe you want to have another one set aside to keep taxes separated out to ensure you will get your estimated taxes paid on time. When using bank accounts, this process can be made automated. This process automates those finances you wish to come out.

For example; if you have a regular payment that comes in you can set up your account to take a certain percentage out of the payment to set aside in another account. This automated process is a great idea for your taxes. If you're doing something like sole proprietorship about 25% of the money that comes in will be going towards your taxes, so you can set up your bank account to take 25% off of any deposit and distribute it into your designated taxes account.

Payments

Once you have gotten your bank accounts set up the next step involves how you're going to accept payments from clients. We live in a modern age where there are a ton of payment options available. Most banks today have their own merchant accounts that you can set up for your payments. Sometimes these options are cheap, and sometimes they are really pricy.

There are always other options such as PayPal, Square, Stripe, and many others. One thing to keep in mind is whether or not you are going to have a storefront operation. Are you going to be meeting clients face to face, or is everything going to be over the phone? With items such as PayPal, and even some merchant accounts, you usually need a device that plugs directly into your smart phone or tablet that allows the ability to accept payments immediately. This is a great way to accept payments while on the go. Most bank accounts also offer a program in which you can take a picture of a check and have it deposited automatically.

If your client wishes to pay by credit card, and you don't have any of these easier means of accepting payments, you can do something like a virtual terminal through your selected bank that allows you to type in the credit card information and charge it then and there. Please be aware that the upcoming EMV update will ship liability for fraudulent transaction to the merchant who swiped or typed in the card number. New credit/debit cards will be issued with chips and merchants will have to dip these cards into a reader to process a transaction.

Money orders are also a possible form of payment. In the case you are dealing with money orders or checks, let your client know that it may take a few business days for this transaction to clear but the process wont start until the money does clear. If you do decide that you want to go ahead and start the process before then, be aware that if the check does not clear and you've already done 30 or so hours of work by that time then you are impeding your business. Be mindful of how you want to handle those types of situations.

In addition to getting your payment methods set up, you need to think about what your time is worth. Are you taking on SEO to replace your current job? Is it your only job? Are you doing it on the side? How much is your time actually worth to you? If you have a family or enjoy going out with friends frequently you need to understand that starting a new business, or even a side business, is going to take up a lot of that time. It is important to think about time versus money management.

For example; if you give up an hour of your family time or an hour of doing something that you really enjoy, how much is that time worth? With this in mind some people would say things like *"I want a million dollars per hour"*, but unfortunately that's not reasonable. Most people would love to charge high prices, but it is more important to determine prices depending on your location. Evaluate your area to see if there are any other local SEO companies. What do their prices look like? Think about what you're getting paid at your current job. Take into account the market that you're targeting for your clients. Are they willing to pay what you intend to charge?

A good number to start off may be 20$/hour or maybe 25$/hour if you're doing hourly rates. You could also do project based pricing where basically you write out a list of items that you're going to perform for a client and then actuate the costs associated with that. Now each client is different so with a project set up like that where you are charging at a static rate, you need to be really specific about what you are willing to do.

You don't want to put anything in there like "I will optimize your entire site" for only $200. If a client comes to you with a 1000 page site and they order the $200 package you're going to be spending so many hours that you're only going to end up being paid pennies on the hour. So when you think about that I would recommend something on an hourly rate or something like a compromise between the two whereas maybe you'll say you will provide training to them for only $50/hour or optimize 5 pages on their site for $300 or whatever your cost is, it's up to you.

In some markets you can charge large amounts in others you will have to charge small amounts. So once you have figured out what exactly you're going to charge you need to think about how you are actually going to be receiving those payments through that bank account and also exactly what are you comfortable doing for a client.

Are you comfortable doing every bit of SEO?

Are you looking at doing some outsourcing?

What does your outsourcer actually provide you?

Contracts

Once you've figured all the information about the services that you're going to offer and the pricing then you can actually look on how to actually get your client to pay, making they pay on time and making sure that they are legally obligated to pay. It's really easy to get into the habit of trusting your clients and having your clients trust you and think you have a good relationship there and then come to find out that they decided that *"Well I don't have the money to pay I'll catch you later"* or *"Well I've decided I'm not going to pay you".* From there it gets really fuzzy and the trust you had breaks really easily and then you feel burned. You might hold that against future clients and then it creates a really bad situation where you're hurting future clients based on your past relationships with clients so it's best to avoid all of that by getting it in a contract.

With contracts you write out exactly what you're doing for a client what the client is obligated to do, what kind of payment they are obligated to pay, when they're obligated to pay it, and you also limit your liability in certain situations. If for some reason the client goes back and destroys the work that you just did, or they have someone else come in and actually go and do extra SEO at the same time as you and that person gets the site blacklisted you don't want that coming back on you. Now you can do a self written contract, have your lawyer write up a contract you should use, or you can use any online services such as Docracy. With Docracy you can use pre-prepared legal documents on the site, or create your own, that are completely legal and binding. It has digital signing so you don't have to worry about faxing documents back and forth and trying to track clients to get them to sign a document. You can easily provide multiple copies to each person and since your contract is online you can pull it up anytime, at any location, you don't have to always be digging through your file cabinet looking for where you have everything stored so it's a great solution for that.

With the contract again make sure you got everything listed out, make sure the pricing is on it and look it over also it helps to have a second eye going over your contract see if you've missed anything. Whether that's a business partner, a significant other, a lawyer or basically anyone that has an outside view to make sure that there isn't anything strange or anything you're forgetting. You can even hire a consultant off of Fiverr or some other place to actually go through the document and make sure you have all your bases covered.

Website

Now once you've figured out your contract information the next thing to consider is a website; how are you actually going to get clients? Are you simply going to call people? Are you going to have a website that actually has your information that you can be tracked to? As an SEO it would be important and even recommended that you would have a website, have all your services listed out if you're targeting a certain market area such as a certain city you might want to get your site ranked for SEO in that city that way people in your city that would be doing searches for SEO or professional SEO or SEO training then your site actually shows up and drive that traffic to it. Also by getting your site a rank for those keywords you can use that as a kind of a proof when you go to a client and say *"We've ranked our own site for the following keywords lets us do the same for you".*

Now on your website you want to do things such as: having a contact form, a lead form, information describing what SEO is, your SEO services, what areas you serve, maybe even offering a free on-page audit/report which you can work up really quick using some software and then provide that to him and say *"Hey Jim, what would be a good time for me to go through this with you?"* and tell him how you can help him. Just like any other business website really helps you with this especially in a digital area like this.

Now that's not to say that you can't do this without a website. You can, however you're probably going to get questioned by your clients about why you don't have your own website. Now once all this is set up you've got a logo for your site you've got maybe business cards printed out or maybe you're doing some marketing by sending out letters. Once you start getting clients in you have to know how to do SEO, so if you're not familiar with SEO it can be kind of daunting about all the information that goes in there. SEO is constantly changing, so you have to really get up to speed and stay up to speed when it comes to that.

What is SEO?

So SEO in its basic form is Search Engine Optimization. What that means you're optimizing content on a site to better rank on search engines and in turn get more traffic to your site. Now that doesn't mean that we're going to write content strictly for search engines just to rank. If we did things like that then the content itself would actually push away the customer that we are going after. So when it comes to actually optimizing the site you have to keep in mind the target audience that you're going after. You have to think about the person that's actually coming to the site, who's actually giving you the money to keep up your site, to keep up your services or if this is your main job, to keep bringing money to you so you can support yourself. So when we optimize a site doing SEO what we're really doing is optimizing it for potential customers, we're optimizing to convert visitors into customers, we're optimizing the content to help us rank on search engines.

Types of SEO

Now there's multiple types of SEO the two main groups are: on-page SEO and off-page SEO. On-page SEO is basically anything on your individual site that you can control and change to help boost your rankings. Off-page SEO is anything not on your site this includes things like social media, pay per click, back links (back links can come in multiple forms they can come in full profile. blog comments, blog posts, plain text links) and article directories. There are so many different types of things that fall into off-page SEO.

Training

Now before you can actually do SEO you have to know how to do SEO and to do that you need to receive training first. This books is going to go over a lot of information a lot of training information but outside of that you have to look into other formats to actually keep up, the book doesn't automatically update you like a computer or a website so you need to find other locations where you can actually find great information on how to SEO and keep up with those changes that are constantly happening.

Now with online information out there you have to be really wary of it. SEO like I said is constantly changing so whenever you are reading an article make sure to check what date that article was posted. If it was posted two years ago it is definitely outdated. In some cases, if it was a couple months ago it can still be outdated, so be really wary and double check information, see if that information is at multiple locations and also you can test out that information, make a quick SEO run and see if it still works.

Places that you can find out more information on SEO and constantly be learning are sites such as Search Engine Land and Moz or even Matt Cutts blog (head of the Google Webspam Team). Each of these places have constant information being added and it'll keep you up to date with the latest information. Sites such as Moz even provide a newsletter that'll send the top ten articles to you that will tell you maybe about test other SEO companies are doing, changes in SEO, as well as individual training to help you learn more about changes that have happened or even past items.

Before Starting SEO

Gather Information from your Client

Now before you even starting SEO, there's a lot of stuff that we actually have to get into. We have to get a lot of information from our client before we can even start creating a plan to actually do their SEO. The first thing we have to do is actually gather that information from that client whether this is a phone call, a document you have written up, or even a face to face conversation with that client.

This is one place where honesty really comes into play. Like I said if you're honest with your client your client is going to be honest with you. Don't let them feel like you're judging them or you're trying to control them. Really sit down, listen to what they're saying, make inferences off that and make sure to clarify where you're uncertain.

So the first thing you want to find out is more about your client's business; what does your client do, is there is a certain target market they go after, do they go after high value clients, do they go after low value clients, do they maybe go after small individual businesses, do they go after major corporations. All this information really comes into play when you start creating your SEO strategy.

You also want to find out if there are certain set of keywords that they want to be listed for or maybe if they have gotten keywords from someone else whether that's another SEO company or maybe even one of their clients said *"hey I found you using this keyword"*. Now you will let them know that you might not be able to use all those keywords but you will consider them in your strategy and that you'll make sure that they get listed for the best possible keywords similar to this. The reason that you will want to let them know this is that if a client gives you a keyword and that word has no traffic, you could list them for this keyword but if there is no traffic basically they're not going to see a return on it and then basically you're wasting their money. So you want to kind of avoid that and make sure to let them that you'll try to use these keywords but you'll let you know why they're not good choices.

The next thing you want to know is if they use social media; do they currently have a Facebook account, a Google plus account, a twitter account, are they keeping up to date with that. You want to find out the URLs for them. That way as you're doing your strategy you can tie social media into that. In addition to that, you also want to find out what other accounts they might have such as do they have something like a Hootsuite account which is used to post on to multiple social media accounts from a single website. We also want to find out information such as do they have a google webmaster tools account, do they have a google analytics account or are they using another analytics program.

You want to find out all this information ahead of time that way you can try and take that information into account maybe there's some information on there that will even help you with your SEO. You also want to find out if they paid anybody in the past for any SEO services. It's really important to find this out because as SEO is constantly changing the person that did SEO at that particular time could have fallen into different categories. They could have been black hat SEOs which might have hurt your client, they could have given bad advice to your client, so now you have to re-educate your client and get them to understand that SEO does change and that information is no longer valid or could even hurt them and get their site blacklisted. You want to find out if somebody else is currently doing SEO services for them, if they are now you get into the point where you need to start talking with that other SEO company and make sure you're not going back over each other and redoing information.

Next you want to find out about what their goal with SEO is. Are they looking to boost visitor to the site? Are they looking to boost their rankings? Are they looking to have more people purchase a product on their website or even simply fill out a form, all this is really going to tie into your SEO strategy? The reason the client is paying you is for you to reach the goals they are setting for themselves and also setting for you. Even if you succeed in another area, if you haven't reached their goal they're not going to be satisfied with it and it also goes back and breaks that kind of trust relationship you've build up with your client.

The next thing you want to look at is, is their goal reasonable, is it something that can reasonably be done either affordably or is it even possible. For example, if someone wants to rank for the term SEO, just the generic term SEO, on google. With SEO you're going to be fighting against millions of other SEO companies and their websites which they may have invested hundreds, thousands, or millions of dollars into actually ranking their sites. In a situation like this if you have a small company and they want to try out rank all these other people it's really just not possible, or even feasible, unless they're devoting a ton of money and a ton of time into it and even then it's definitely not guaranteed.

The next thing you want to let your client know is that with SEO what you're doing is you're doing a best case scenario where basically you're doing your best to improve their chances of ranking but there's no guarantee in SEO. One of the things I like to tell my client is that I will guarantee I'll do my best to help you rank better but I can't guarantee you a certain spot or a certain number of visitors and the reason I can't is it's impossible to guarantee that. If somebody else does guarantee that to you then more than likely they're not being honest with you they're basically telling you something in order to get your money.

I recommend telling your client *"I'm not simply trying to take your money, I want to help you reach that goal but at the same time I want to make sure you understand that I can't work magic. What I can do is help you get your site better optimized to actually rank higher on the search engines to help drive more traffic to you from other sources."*

The next thing you want to do, and this is actually something you should be constantly doing, is to educate your client. A client that is not educated won't be able to understand what you're doing for them, and they won't understand how you're better than another SEO provider. The other thing too is the more that you help your client to understand what SEO is what you can offer them, the more business they're going to bring too you not only from themselves but from other people. If you do a great job for somebody they are going to let other people know that this guy did an amazing SEO on my website, he boosted my rankings, boosted my traffic and I would recommend him to you.

So as you make those changes you're going to let the client know why you are making those changes. In the case of you changing meta tags or your changing their key words and you're not using the original key words you'll let them know why that's happening. That way they'd understand what's going on and it increase that trust with you, you're being honest with them about each individual phase of SEO. They will understand that you are an expert in that field and you're looking out for their best interest.

The next thing you want to do is find out their budget. Do they have a large budget for SEO? Are they looking to pay a flat rate fee one time to do some small SEO and they don't want to do anything else? Or do they have a large budget that basically will let you do everything? Some clients may want to do some of this on their own where you charge them a training fee to teach them in a little bit of SEO and then you perform the hard stuff for them. These are items such as HTML changes, backlink building, fixing broken links. It all comes back to that budget can they afford the services that you're going to provide. If cases where they can't afford it, try to be flexible. Let's say typically you charge something like $300 or $3000 but the client only has $100 or $1000. Let them know that's not what you usually work for but for them you will build a custom package that fits their budget. That way you're not sending away a customer but at the same time you're doing it from a financial stand point that impacts you and actually gets you the funds. This way you're not over working yourself and being unpaid for it.

Paperwork and Payments

The next stage is where you go ahead and start a plan for that client. You will look at on page optimization and ask yourself: do we need to look at link building, are we doing social media management reputation management, are we doing local SEO as well? Find out all the bits and pieces of what you want to do and write that out. Maybe you segregate it out and say something similar to the following:

"For the first month I'll tackle your on page issues. We'll build a nice foundation for your future SEO by doing that and in the next month we'll start on things such as adding content. We'll do social media for you followed by local SEO and get that optimized."

Perhaps you'll be charging the client to write content for them. All of this will go into a plan and that way you know also how much you'll actually be charging and how you're going to be using that money effectively. The next thing is you're going to get a contract together that covers all these items. Make sure everything is outlined, make sure there's no grey areas that people might take it one way and you meant it another way. Once you have that contract together get it to the client have them sign it, make sure both of you sign it. Both of you should have a copy whether it's a physical contract or an electronic contract say through Docracy or another website.

For payment you want to receive your payment upfront. With SEO, all the changes that you are doing, these are changes once they're done it's not something you can simply turn off because the client didn't pay you. The changes have already been done. You've done all this work so if you get half upfront, half later, and then the client doesn't pay then you are out the money and they still have the fruits of your labor. So, with SEO, typically it's best to let the client know that when it comes to SEO the payment is upfront and if you do it through something like PayPal you can let them know that *"I'm using PayPal for payments, this protects both parties making sure that I do what I'm supposed to do, but at the same time that I receive the payment for all my hard work".*

Once you receive that payment make sure you give the client a receipt back. Make sure you're doing some kind of invoice with this, whether it's through a service such as FreshBooks or QuickBooks some kind of accounting software. Once you've actually received your payment you can start on your SEO.

Performing SEO

The Research Stage

The very first step before any SEO work actually happens is actually doing your keyword research. This can be very time intensive, which means it can also cost a lot of money. If your client has keywords that have been previously researched by someone else, you can do a quick check just to see if they're good keywords. If they are then great! Those are words you can immediately use to help your client.

When it comes to keyword research there's a lot of tools that can actually help out with this. You can do a very basic one manually if you don't have the money for tools.

The Manual Method

This can be accomplished doing a Google Keyword Planner search. You put in your keywords and do a quick search to find information on your words and alternatives.

Make sure check off which area you're targeting if you're going after US make sure you select US.

After you have the results; look at the amount of traffic and the competition that's listed there on google and determine what you can go after. What I'd recommend is looking at the results and if the traffic is high enough and the keywords are not too broad (such as if someone is going after the word SEO). Then I would look at further analyzing the results. Check if you've got a good level of traffic, the competition is low to medium. If the site is just starting out they might be able to rank for these. Or if it's a high competition keyword and you think that the website can actually compete for a high competition keyword based on its age, traffic levels, or other factors.

The next thing you'll look at is the actual competitors. The easiest way to do this is to actually use a browser plug in such as SEO Quake for Firefox and opening up a private window. The reason why it's important to use a private window is that when Google considers rankings it considers a ton of factors and your google account can play into that. Google has the ability to look at your previous emails your previous search history, your social media accounts such as Google+. A lot of information with each of those that can impact those rankings and other things like geolocation also come into play. I can't say for certain geolocation is taken out of the picture when it comes to using a private location; that's probably still in there based on your IP address. But a private window can help to minimize a lot of the other factors.

Now, with SEO Quake, you perform a Google search for

your keyword and it will display a toolbar for each of the search results. It's going to give you really important information such as the page rank and the number of backlinks to the individual pages, the links for the domain itself, and more. You can use it to check out the optimization level for each of those pages. You can look and see how old the website is and to see if your client has a chance of ranking against them.

For example, let's say that the listings have a lot of information for Moz.com. Now this is and example for the SEO keyword, but let's say there are listings for Moz.com, Search Engine Land, or really big players in the search engine area. If our client is a start-up company, they're not going to be able to outrank these people. But let's say you try to go for a keyword like *affordable SEO companies in Michigan* and the top result are from every local companies or maybe for a Facebook page. With results like this, you know you can outrank those pages with a little bit of work. As long as they are not really high quality, with a ton of backlinks, and high page rank level. In cases like that you know the keyword is a good choice.

So you do want to go and do that research for each possible keyword from your list. If you have the money, you can use tools to actually help you with this research and make it a little bit easier where it's not so manual.

Using Paid Tools

You can use tools such as Rank Tracker, which is part of the SEO Power Suite. You can use Moz's tools. You can use Market Samurai, Long Tail Pro, or RavenTools. There are so many different tools out there that can with keyword research. With each of them you will take your list of key words, enter them, and they will tell you how competitive that individual keyword is and what your chance of ranking that keyword are based on that.

And of course with any tools, use your own personal intuition your personal knowledge to actually determine if what that tool is saying is actually something that makes sense or if you think that the tool is actually giving you the proper information. The tool is only as good as the person using the tool.

Baseline Analysis

Once you have your list of usable keywords you can actually perform your SEO. To perform the SEO you want to start by getting a base line of where that website stands. You want to do this by doing a Site Audit or basically look at the content on their site. You're going to look for those things such as broken links. You're going to look for over optimization. So many different factors come under this area. There's a lot a tools to help you with this.

The one we recommend would be Website Auditor which is part of the SEO Power Suite tool set. With this you basically put in your URL, let it run through, and it pulls out all the information for you. It even creates a wonderful looking report that you can then give to your client as an extra service. Or even use as kind of a marketing tactic to pull in new clients say *"Hey here's a report we did of your site. Let us explain how we can help you fix these issues"*.

You can also do an on page optimization check for

keywords. If a client says they are targeting a certain keyword on this page, you can analyze that page for the optimization. With Website Auditor it'll actually tell you where that keyword is being used at and the different areas you might want to optimize even more. You will also see how well the competition is actually optimized in those areas as well. You can create a massive report that's great for showing the client and it's also great for your future checks.

The next thing you want to look at is a backlink report. You want to check and see if your website actually has backlinks and the quality of those backlinks. Again, there's a ton of tools out there for this. If you're using the SEO Power Suite you would use SEO SpyGlass. There are websites such as LinkQuidator, there's stuff on Moz, there are so many different tools out there for this.

Basically what you're looking at is the quality of these backlinks and where the links come from. Let's say the client lives in the US and most of these website linking to them in the US this is great. Or they have stuff coming from Russia or Ukraine or places where the quality of that just isn't that great. Maybe the page that links to them has a ton of links, or Google is penalizing that site. These bad links could in turn hurt your client, so you want to see what is helping or hurting the site. That will also let you know what other service you may want to offer to your client to fix these issues and possibly rank better.

You also want to look at their actual page itself. Tools aren't always going to pick up certain things such as hidden content or places where they've really over optimized the content. A good example is keyword density. Keyword

Density basically means how many times that keyword appears in the text of a website. It used to be that people would use the keyword over and over again and it would cause a site to boost its rankings even higher but this would look really spammy. You would basically see the word, for example again SEO, multiple times and you might even see sentences and paragraphs that look something like *"are you looking for affordable SEO our SEO consultants are the best SEO performers in this area, buy our SEO services and we will perform SEO on your site using our affordable SEO services".* It's a very spammy method and you'll still see that being used in certain locations.

Keyword density is a percentage, it used to be recommended about 3-4% which of course the example is way over that but 3-4% was recommended. These days, something like 1%, a very natural looking use of keywords, is more recommended. When it comes to optimizing content and there's a lot of better ways to do that than spamming your keyword.

The next thing is hidden content, hidden content is where they have some text on the site but they hide it from showing up. A good way to test for this is to press Ctrl + A or ⌘ + A on your keyboard and then look for areas where text shows up where it didn't before. This tactic was where people would hide text from showing up, and typically it would be a lot of their keywords, and search engine would see it but it doesn't look so spammy to visitors. Of course search engines know that this happens and can determine if content is hidden and it'll hurt the client by having that.

The next thing to tackle is broken links. If there's a link

on your site that goes to a page that no longer exists, like n outside website that shut down, then that link is considered broken. When Google and other search engines index a site, they start going through it by starting at the homepage and following each link to find individual pages on your site. If they come across a link that doesn't lead them anywhere it's a broken link. The website you are linking to might no longer exist, or maybe you misspelled a link to a page on your site, or even deleted the page.

These kind of links get flagged and search engines will leave the site and come back later to check for a proper link. Its almost as if they say *"Hey look we hit a broken link! We'll come back later and see if they got it fixed."*. Now, if that happens over and over again, what google and other search engines might defer from that is: maybe you're not updating you content, maybe you don't care about actually fixing those issues, maybe you just haven't been on the site in long time, or maybe the sites out of date. This is why it's really important to get those links fixed. It may even impact your rankings. We don't know the specifics of the google search algorithm or Bing's search algorithm but it's one more thing you should go ahead and fix. Its just one more issue that you that might be hurting you.

The next is those backlinks, double checking make sure they're not bad backlinks. If they are bad backlinks, then you want to look at fixing these issues as well as the other issues.

To fix the issues, you want to look at your content, if the content is over optimized you want to get that content rewritten. If you have broken links you want to go and fix those broken links. Maybe someone mistyped the URL, you can go and you fix that. Maybe the website you're linking to doesn't exist anymore, you just want to remove that link.

You want to work your way down your report, fixing each of these individual issues. When it comes to things like HTML errors, you have what is called **W3C HTML Validator and CSS Validator** and tools such as **Website Auditor**. The numbers listed on these tools can be confusing. I recommend checking them as sometimes you see what is called false positive. This happens in cases where the code on the page is legitimate code, that is in use, but it's not on the list of things that the validator approves of. For example, things like the Facebook Open Graph tags and the Twitter Card tags will usually be shown as a HTML error. It's being used by Facebook but since its not in the list the validators check it shows as an error.

So, on your Website Auditor report, if a page shows there's fifty errors, then you want to click and double check those errors. Maybe it's things such as the open graph tags that are contributing to some of these errors or it might be actual legitimate errors. Maybe they've got HTML text overlap, or maybe they forgot the ATL text on an image. See what shows up and let your client know that there may be false positives. After you've done the actual fixes and you rerun your report, walk through these areas with the client and let them know which ones are false positives.

For bad backlinks you want to look at if you need to disavow your backlinks. When it comes to backlinks you can ask if the website owner if they can/will remove your backlink to try and get rid of that bad backlink. If this fails, you can disavow bad links by using Google's disavow tool. In some cases, the client might know where these links came from, perhaps they purchased a Fiverr gig for backlinks. Alternatively, somebody might have sent bad backlinks to their site on purpose to try and hurt your client or associate them with bad things. Maybe they did porn links or really spammy links or they're just trashing their company on other places. You can disavow those links and say *"hey I didn't do these links they're hurting me please ignore these"* and basically google will stop carrying those bad backlinks against you.

Notes on making changes

And one other final note we want to make when it comes to HTML changes is how to actually perform those HTML fixes. If it's a self-coded website, like a static HTML site or a static PHP site, you can go and make those changes directly in the code. If they are using a CMS such as WordPress or Drupal then you're probably using a theme. Typically, these can receive updates and you don't want to make your changes directly in that main theme. If you do then what will happen is that any HTML fixes you make will be overwritten if that theme is updated.

In the case of WordPress, and if another solution supports it, you want to use something like a child theme. A child theme is a theme that says *"hey I'm a child of this theme, I can overwrite the following, but if I don't overwrite it use what my parent theme says"*. That way you're not redoing everything from scratch, but you are fixing those individual issues. The other thing too, is once updates happen your child theme still functions and all your fixes are still in place.

After an update, you might have to fix some issues. For example, if a new feature was added or major code changes happen. You're not losing all the hard work you've put into place; you just have to update your own child theme to keep up with the parent theme.

Beginning the Changes

This next section will try and tackle both hard coded HTML sites as well as popular CMS solutions such as WordPress and Drupal.

Working with Content Management Systems

Now speaking of WordPress, or other CMSs, you can actually get plugins that help you with SEO. So, as you're starting with SEO, and actually performing SEO, optimization plugins will help you optimize that content. You don't have to memorize absolutely every step that you have to perform to optimize the content. It's really helpful when you're starting out.

For WordPress there're plugins such as Yoast SEO. This helps with on-page optimization of your content, it helps with site maps, it helps with social media tags, and a lot of similar things. If you don't use Yoast, then maybe you would go with something like SEO Ultimate or SEOPressor. A lot of tools other than Yoast don't include the ability to generate site maps. A site map is a representation of all the pages on your site in XML format. XML format is a specially coded format that can be used by other sites. It can be used by

Google Webmaster Tools and Bing Webmaster Tools to notify them of all the pages on your site. They can then look at that content and actually see when things have been added and how often it's being updated. Without a site map plugin WordPress usually does not create a sitemap.xml file so you want to make sure you use a plugin for that. If you're using Yoast, just make sure that feature is turned on.

In addition to on page optimization plugins there's other optimizations you can do. You can use something such as Smush.it which compresses your files, whether it's images or other files, into a smaller file size so they load faster. Site load time is a new SEO factor so if you compress the size of your images the site will load even faster which will help boost your rankings and in turn visitors. The other thing that will help improve site load time is a cash in plugin such as W3TotalCache which create a cached version which is to say a static copy of your content at a single point in time. Typically, whenever a page is loaded on a WordPress website there's a lot of stuff happening in the background. The system has to generate all of the page content, do all the styling, and process short codes or plugin information to actually generate that page. This happens every time, and sometimes that can take a long time to actually do.

Your browser or a customer's browser actually does some caching, but you can make it even better by doing it at the server level. So, with W3TotalCache it basically makes a copy of the pages that are loading at certain times and then displays that copy for a short time which is much faster than regenerating everything.

One other thing; with SEOPressor, this is another on

page optimization plugin, you have to be careful with plugins like this because it's very easy to over optimize your content. When you start to optimize your content using a plugin you are given a list of items to perform. As you do each one the item will turn green or become "checked off". It's very easy to forget that you're actually targeting an actual person not just search engines. It's best to remember that these items are recommendations and along the way you should ask yourself *"Does this change look natural? AM I doing this just to check off a box or does it make sense?"*.

HTML Sites

Now we talked about content management systems such as WordPress or Drupal, but you can also have hard coded sites or maybe just static HTML site. When it comes to these, there're still changes you can make to help optimize these. You can do actual changes and use something like a .htaccess file to enable some caching or gzip the content going over the connection to your visitor's browser.

There's a lot of other items that can go into these optimizations but with hard code sites you are kind of at a disadvantage sometimes. That's because you have to know that much more about coding and SEO to actually get this done. The other thing too is when it comes to making changes with a static HTML site, if it's completely static HTML, that means that every file contains a copy of your header, footer, menu, and other layout elements. Instead of you making HTML fixes in a theme file or a single menu file, you're now making the same changes across all the pages of your site.

If you're working on a PHP and HTML site then more than likely your web developer, or you, have probably made the smart decision of actually segregate those areas. If you did then there are usually individual files such as a header or footer file where that content is in one location and in each of the other pages includes a header and a footer. This way you're only making those changes one time and it affects all the pages. So just make sure that when you're doing these things, you do it from a smart perspective and use what's available to you to make your job that much easier.

Handling Reorganization Properly

As we are doing SEO and optimize we're adding content or even moving it to a different location. It's really important that we consider redirects when we decide to move pages. What I mean by that is that if you have a piece of content that is out there and its either important or an old page with links to you have to move the content properly. If you suddenly change the URL or you delete that page, all the links this page stop working. If someone tries to come to that page they will typically see and error page or a 404 error screen. This means that any backlinks you had built for it are worthless and you're losing any traffic from the search indexes or these links.

To do this properly you'll need to create what's called a 301 redirect. A 301 redirect is a piece of code that says *"my content is moved, you'll find it here"*. This is very easily to do if you're using a Content Management System. There are plugins to do this for you; some of the plugins don't always work so it's also good to know the manual way of doing this. The manual way of doing this is by using a .htaccess file.

There's a ton of information out there on the internet using a simple google search, but you can find a great example here: PLACE_A_LINK_HERE.

The typical situations you will use a 301 are for: fixing 404 errors, moving content, combining pages, or for switching domain names. One reason you might move the content during SEO is to fully optimize a page. One of the recommendations to optimize a page is to the keyword in the page URL. For example, lets say you want to optimize the About Us on your website. Typically, your URL for this page looks like: mysite.com/aboutus. This gets the point across but its not really optimized. A better solution would be to use mysite.com/about-my-company-name. Once the page has been renamed we need to fix any links on our site to point to the new page and create a 301 redirect. This is done for two reasons. The first is that any website on the internet that tries to come to that page will be redirected to the new one. The second is that in cases where we missed a link on the site, a visitor will still be redirected.

You can find a cheat sheet for various types of redirects on this blog post: 301 redirects or Properly Moving Pages with .htaccess.

Optimizing the Page Content

This is your real first step in performing on page SEO, everything else so far has been a framework of sorts. Pick a page on your site that you want to optimize. You want to look at the content that's there and make sure that you're getting the most out of it. Each page should be optimized for a specific keyword phrase or theme. Decide now which keyword you are going to optimize the page for. If you're using a plugin such as Yoast, this is really easy there's a section that walks you through optimization and it's the same optimization that you would do if you're doing this manually. For Yoast, just enter your chosen keyword and save the page. This will update all the SEO factors and it will walk you through it.

When optimizing a page, we're taking their keyword, as well as related or synonymous topics, and we're using it in strategic locations. We're using it in the page title, meta description, the H1 and possibly the H2 through H6 tags. <u>We're not using meta keywords because it's not used by search engines and it only proves to give other people our keywords.</u> We're using them in the body of the content; preferably in the first sentence and the last sentence. We also want to use it on any images by including it in the filename and the alt text attribute. When we do use it on images, we want to make sure that image is actually related to our keyword because we don't want to have a picture of a dog and call it SEO company.

But if it is let's say the image is your own business building, you could use "My SEO company office" and there your keyword is actually in that alternate text, it matches the image, and you're not doing it for spamming purposes. If it makes sense in the body of the content you can do things like bolding, italicizing or underlining. You don't want to do these just to mark them off a list but if it makes sense, and looks like a natural call, then by all means feel free to do that. This can result in a small boost to your SEO and in turn rankings.

You can also use links to external authority sites or related site in your niche. This is done for two reasons. The first is that it shows search engines that you are providing additional resources for visitors. Secondly, it allows anyone coming to your site to find not only the information you provide but also other places which might have more info. Doing this can result in a small boost to your SEO. These links can point to another page on your site or a Wikipedia article.

With Yoast, these items cover the basic things that show on there. But, whenever you use a tool like this or SEOPressor, you want to ask yourself: *"Does it make sense for me to do this item on the list? If I do this, does it look natural to search engines?".* What you're basically asking yourself is if you doing this just to make myself rank higher or am I doing this because it helps the person coming to the site. Your final goal should be the latter. If somebody comes to the site and they can't understand what's on there, it's not helpful or friendly to them and they're going to leave and go somewhere else that might be a little friendlier.

That's the basic process for optimizing individual pages, simply add your content and the optimize for the chosen keyword by using it in the specified locations. This process is for both the main pages of your site such as the home page, services page, product pages, and can also be used on blog posts. If a site doesn't have a blog you should really consider adding it. Search engines are always checking a site for fresh content and log is a very easy way to meet these expectations. In addition, a blog allows you to share that content out and also drives traffic to your internal pages.

Conversion Rate Optimization

Next we should consider Conversion Rate Optimization. This means that in addition to optimizing your content for search engines, you optimize it for your visitors. This means we choose a single goal for a page and then do what we can to make sure that goal is accomplished. This can be getting visitors to purchase a product, submit a form, or sign up for a newsletter. Conversion Rate Optimization is basically saying *"On this page my goal is the following.... What do I need to do to make that goal happen?"*. To do this, we need to look into A/B split testing.

A/B split testing is creating two slightly different views of a page. You should make a single change at a time and then analyze it to see if it works. For example, you can change the text of a button from **Buy Now** to **Get This Today**. You then wait a week a more and compare the conversions you saw on version A vs version B. If the changed version got more purchases, then you know that it's a change you should keep. If you lost conversions, then you know the original version is better.

There are a lot of factors you can test. Some of these can be simply items such as the text example above, the color of items, prices, the pictures on a page, or even just the layout. Other larger tests can be items such as changing the full page text, creating a basic landing page, the location of the call to action, and others.

Ads or Pay Per Click Campaigns

Depending on your client's budget, you might be able to suggest starting an ad campaign. These can include physical ads such as newspapers, periodicals, mailing flyers, and/or digital ads. For the purpose of this book we will focus on the latter. Just remember that businesses can profit from all of these channels so we recommend researching these other methods as well.

When we talk about ads people typically thing of Google AdWords. This is a good solution but there are other options such as Bing Ads, Facebook Ads, and purchasing ads on other companies' websites. Ad tools such as Google AdWords allow you to specify the keywords you want to be shown for, demographics such as location, the cost per click, and the ad text itself. For example, in Google AdWords we can specify that we want to go after the keyword "SEO" in the United States, pay less that $2 per click, and our ad text is:

SEO Services

Get professional SEO today.

Great prices, great service.

http://www.oursite.com

Google has specific limitation on how much text we are allowed to use here. They are as follows:

- Title cannot be longer than 25 characters
- Each description line cannot longer than 35 characters
- The link cannot longer than 35 characters

Other services such as Bing Ads or Facebook Ads have their own rules.

When choosing which service to utilize there are a lot of factors to choose such as reach, cost, and impact. Facebook Ads allows a great middle ground for all of these and is typically the method we recommend. For ads you get a larger area for title, longer descriptions, and the ability to use images. You also can be even more specific with your demographics. You can enter factors such as age, browsing habits, specific interests, and can even go as far as targeting one specific user. In addition to this the cost for Facebook ads is typically cheaper than the version on Google or Bing.

We recommend analyzing all of the options in each case to determine which service would work best for your client's specific needs.

Keeping Track of Clients and Reporting

Now as far as tools go when you're doing SEO there are simple options such as Excel and complex Project Management tools which allow you to keep track of the items you have on your plate for each client. If you only have one client at a time, it's fairly easy to keep track of tasks on a sticky note. But, when you start getting multiple clients, it's very easy to get overwhelmed.

If you decide to go with an excel document to track tasks you can create a sheet that handles the individual tasks and which client, they go to. This allows you see what's on your plate and have the ability to easily reorganize at any time. You can combine this with the built in calendar feature on most computers to carve out a specific time each day to work on tasks as well as keeping track of due dates.

You can also use excel to create invoice for your clients when you are first starting off.

A better solution would be to use an online Project Management system. This allows you to keep track of tasks no matter where you are. Most online tools also allow customizations or plugins to expand easily. A good example of this would be a Fast Track Sites SEO Management System. It's an affordable tool that fits most budgets and walks you through additional SEO beyond this book. With this tool, you enter the client's website and it provides checklist items to walk you through optimizing everything from doing local SEO, basic reputation management, and backlinks. The nice thing about this tool is that you can add your own items which show up for all clients. You can also contact the developer if a feature isn't available and typically a developer would go and add extra features as long as enough clients want that feature.

Paid Subscription Tools

With many SEO tools other than the one above, you're typically paying a monthly cost to utilize them. In the SEO business we tend to use a multitude of tools and these costs can add up. Many tools start at a rate of $99 per month for the cheapest packages and have a limitation on the number of sites you can add or reports you can run. Social Media Management (SMM) software can be expensive but one of the cheapest options here is to manage your own using a tool such as Hootsuite.

Hootsuite is a tool where you sign in and link it to your social media accounts which allows you to manage all of them from a single website. You can schedule posts, utilize images, import posts, and much more. There are paid plans and free plans; the latter will add a *"Posted using Hootsuite"* message to the bottom of your posts. As a SEO company, if you're doing social media management, you probably don't have the time to sign into all of your client's individual accounts, make a post, log out, log back in, and repeat. It just takes up too much time. That's why tools such as Hootsuite are a great help.

The scheduling feature works in two ways. The included version allows you to enter your post and then Hootsuite determines the best time to actually post it to each account based on factors such as previous engagement. The other, which is a paid add-on, allows you to upload an excel file listing out the individual posts, accounts, dates, and time and then Hootsuite will post these when needed. This allows you to schedule out an entire week of posts, or more, ahead of time.

If you aren't doing SMM, maybe the client doesn't have enough money or they're doing it themselves, you can also pay outside companies to do it for them. One example is 99DollarSocial, which will manage the social media account for you for an affordable fee. Even if you are doing the actual management, you might find you want to outsource it to a company like that were you might get a kick back based on that fee. This allows you to use your time for other things such as reporting and research.

If you are doing your own SEO and providing the reports to the client, there're a lot of software options out there. Most of these are web based tools, but there's also a well known one you can install on your system: SEO Power Suite. This is a tool set that has an upfront cost and then a recurring cost to keep up with algorithm changes made by search engines. It has a vast assortment of reporting features built in. You can get reports on: site wide issues, on page optimization reporting, backlinks for a clients site, backlinks for competitors, keyword rankings, keyword research reports, and also contact other webmasters for backlinks.

There is a free trial of the software available here which allows you to test the software before committing to it. With reporting software, you not only gain a professional method to report issues and changes to clients, you also gain a way to recoup the software costs. You can choose to sell the reports or consultation services to go over the issues located therein.

For online tools that you can try, there is Moz, SEMRush, Raven SEO Tools, Ahrefs, and Linkquidator just to list a few. Moz offers an amazing tool set for a monthly fee. They have keyword research tools, backlink analysis, and an in depth reporting and ranking tracking system. They also run an in depth and constantly updated blog which is a great source of information when it comes to training. Raven SEO Tools, which is a new tool, has a great set of reporting tools and also offers page optimization from a variety of angles.

For SEMRush, it's a great site to do research revolving around on a pay per click as well as keywords you and your competition rank for. You can quickly get competition and search analysis metrics to determine what you need to improve upon. Ahrefs is a site for looking at links, it's a great way to check and see if you're over optimized for link or anchor text. It will also tell you if you have good diversity between you links or if all your links are coming from bad locations. You can use this to also look at competitors linking structure and maybe even copy some of their links. Linkquidator this is a great tool for analyzing your own backlinks and then picking up which links are bad or hurting you. This information can be used to disavow bad links and keep them from hurting you. These are only a small subsection of the possible tools that are out; new tools are constantly being added, so keep up with it!

Backlinks

What They Are, and Why We Want Them

A backlink is simply a link on any site on the internet that points back to your website. This includes links on social media, article directories, forums, and other sites. Each of these links can drive traffic to your website and in turn bring in more customers. These links are also a metric that search engines use in order to determine how to rank you on the search results. We want to have high quality links from reputable sites that are preferably in the same niche as us.

Never buy links! There are few situations where this may be acceptable, but search engines look down on it. There are a lot of factors that would go into determining if the cost is worth the benefit but its much simpler to simply avoid buying links. This include links from Fiverr gigs or another site that you simply found.

How to Get Them

To get a backlink there are a multitude of ways to find and get a link. The two min ways are: copying a competitor's backlinks and researching your own links.

Copying Competitor's Backlinks

Your competitors are performing SEO just like you, even if they aren't paying someone to do it. Each post they add to their site, every link they get, each social media page; all of these fall under SEO. An easy way to find a new backlink is by checking where your competitors get theirs. This is as simple as using SEO SpyGlass, SEMRush, Ahrefs, or another tool to generate a list of links that point to a website. We like to get a list of links for around 8 of the competitors for a keyword and organize them in Excel. From here we want to look at factors such as if the site has too many links, what type of link our competitor received, and if we can even get a link from that page.

For the analysis part of this, many of the tools above will list a Link Value or Spam Score for the links. If the value is high or the spam score is low, it might be a good option. Thankfully, Excel has the ability to filter data so let's start by filtering out any data that falls outside the scores we are looking for. Next let's look at the anchor text and pre anchor text fields that we typically find on the reports.

Let's say we are in the web design niche and our competitor is XYZ Company. If a link on our report says something like *"Website Designed By: XYZ Company"* we know that this is typically a link in the footer of a website and we can't get that link. In many cases you'll see this same link across the entire website. Most web design companies use this tactic.

If you see an anchor text that says *Image*, then this means the backlink is attached to an image. This will typically mean that it is an ad on the site or its an image in the body of the text. This means we might be able to get a backlink here.

Next we should look at the country that the website is in. If we are a US based business we typically want links from US based websites. If we instead had a lot of overseas links, our backlinks would look unnatural.

Once we've filtered out any bad links we now have to start the slow process of visiting each page and checking for a few things. One is if there is a comments section. If there is then we can add a relevant comment to the page and provide our website information to receive a backlink. These types of backlinks don't help as much as they used to, but its better than no link at all.

Next is if there is no comments section and, lets say our competitor's backlink is in the article body, we can try and contact the website owner to see if they would consider writing an article about us. This tactic is useful in situations where the article was a review, the competitor was on a *Top 10* style list, or in situations where we don't see another way of getting a link here.

If we have to manually contact the site's owner then we should determine how an article about our company would help the website, and how it would help us as well. Sometimes owners will do this for free, and other times there may be a small fee.

Researching Your Own Backlinks

To find new backlink opportunities, we can use our good friend Google. If we know we want to rank for a specific keyword we can use any of the search queries below and find possible sites to add our own link to.

- blog + intitle:"keyword" OR inurl:"keyword"
- article + intitle:"keyword" OR inurl:"keyword"
- directory + intitle:"keyword" OR inurl:"keyword"
- website + intitle:"keyword" OR inurl:"keyword"
- links + intitle:"keyword" OR inurl:"keyword"
- roundup + intitle:"keyword" OR inurl:"keyword"
- guide + intitle:"keyword" OR inurl:"keyword"
- tag + intitle:"keyword" OR inurl:"keyword"
- news + intitle:"keyword" OR inurl:"keyword"
- magazine + intitle:"keyword" OR inurl:"keyword"
- resource + intitle:"keyword" OR inurl:"keyword"
- research + intitle:"keyword" OR inurl:"keyword"
- write for us + intitle:"keyword" OR inurl:"keyword"
- guest blog + intitle:"keyword" OR inurl:"keyword"
- guest blogger + intitle:"keyword" OR inurl:"keyword"
- guest column + intitle:"keyword" OR inurl:"keyword"
- guest article + intitle:"keyword" OR inurl:"keyword"
- become a contributor + intitle:"keyword" OR inurl:"keyword"

- guest author + intitle:"keyword" OR inurl:"keyword"

- guest post + intitle:"keyword" OR inurl:"keyword"

- contribute to our + intitle:"keyword" OR inurl:"keyword"

- contribute to this + intitle:"keyword" OR inurl:"keyword"

These searches should give us a fair share of sites where we can submit articles to the site or provide a nice comment. Some of these site will allow you to provide what's called a guest blog post. This is where you write the article and they post it on their site with a short bio about you and your company. Typically, you are allowed a few links within the article. This helps the website owner gain visits by having fresh content, and it helps you by giving your site a great backlink that is relevant to your niche.

In addition to these searches we should also look at sites such as Foursquare, Yelp, and Google Places. These are great places to get backlinks for Local Citations. You do not have to own a Brick and Mortar business to get listed here, you can use your home address and simply hide it. Many businesses are now what are referred to as "service businesses" or "regional businesses". These businesses are where you service a client's needs at their home or another location. A freelancer is a good example of this

What to Watch Out For

There are a lot of services out there that promise a large number of backlinks for very little work and cost. You should avoid these as typically the links are created using a software that doesn't care where the website comes from, what the quality is, or if it will hurt the site it links to. They only care that they can provide a link.

You will typically see services like this on Fiverr or other sites and they come in many forms. A few of these are listed below:

1. Link Pyramid
2. Link Wheel
3. Forum Profile Backlinks
4. SENuke
5. Article Directory Submission
6. Website Directory Submission
7. Press Release Submission

Some of these items are acceptable if you take the time to do them manually. The issue with the cheaper services is that the same text and link are being spammed to multiple sites. Its much better to choose good sites and make the submissions manually.

Wrapping Things Up

truly hope you enjoyed this book and that it has helped you get closer to running your own SEO business. If there's something you don't understand, feel free to take a look at our site for more information. Below, you will find a mind map which walks through a lot of the processes of doing SEO. You can use it as you get new clients and follow long each step to make sure you don't miss anything. Everything in SEO does change, so make sure to keep up the new training.

Good luck with SEO, and good luck with your new SEO business!

Resources

We have crated a special website to list all of the resources and tools we've mentioned in this book. This allows us to constantly update the list and provide you with any discounts our partners have going at the time.

https://www.fasttracksites.com/build-your-own-seo-business-resources/

www.ingramcontent.com/pod-product-compliance
Lightning Source LLC
LaVergne TN
LVHW052321060326
832902LV00023B/4522